CORD[ ]

TRAVEL GUIDE

2024

The Ultimate Guide to Discovering the Beautiful Sights, History, Food and Culture of Cordoba.

Tormes Rivera.

INTRODUCTION

As the plane touched down on Cordoba's sun-kissed runway, I could feel the anticipation building within me. The whispers of history and the echoes of cultures past seemed to linger in the air, promising a journey unlike any other. Little did I know, Cordoba held secrets waiting to be unveiled, and my adventure began the moment I stepped off the plane.

The airport, though modern and bustling, held a certain mystique. It was as if the walls themselves whispered tales of travelers who had passed through, each one leaving a trace of their own story. But there was one story that had always intrigued me—the story of Cordoba's transformation.

Once upon a time, Cordoba was not just a city; it was a jewel in the crown of Al-Andalus, the heart of Muslim Spain. The airport, where I stood, was once the very gateway to this extraordinary civilization. As I made my way towards the baggage claim, I couldn't help but imagine the scene when Cordoba was the world's largest and most advanced city, a beacon of knowledge, art, and coexistence.

My curiosity led me to explore beyond the airport's sleek architecture. Just a short drive away lay the Mezquita-Catedral, an architectural marvel that bore witness to the city's rich history. This breathtaking structure was the embodiment of Cordoba's transformation. Once a grand mosque, it had been converted into a cathedral after the Christian Reconquista. The melding of two faiths in a single building was a testament to Cordoba's complex tapestry of history.

The Mezquita-Catedral's interior was a sensory overload. A sea of red and white arches stretched out before me, a mesmerizing display of Moorish and Christian architecture coexisting in harmony. The play of light and shadow was enchanting, as if the building itself held secrets in its patterns.

My journey continued through the narrow cobblestone streets of the city's historic center. Cordoba's patios, adorned with vibrant flowers, transported me to a different time. Each patio seemed to have a story of its own, a tale of passion and pride that was shared during the annual Patio Festival.

But it was the aroma of Cordoba's cuisine that truly ensnared my senses. I found myself in a tiny tavern, where I indulged in a traditional Andalusian feast. The flavors of salmorejo, a creamy tomato and bread soup, and rabo de toro, tender oxtail stew, danced on my taste buds. It was a culinary journey that resonated with the city's diverse history.

Cordoba's enchantment extended beyond its landmarks and flavors; it was in the warmth of its people. As I strolled along the Guadalquivir River, I struck up a conversation with a local artist. His passion for Cordoba's culture was infectious, and he invited me to his studio, where he painted with the fervor of someone deeply connected to his roots.

The sun dipped below the horizon, casting a warm glow over the city. I watched as Cordoba transformed once more, this time into a city of lights. The Mezquita-Catedral illuminated the night sky, a radiant symbol of Cordoba's enduring spirit.

My journey had only just begun, and Cordoba had already woven its spell around me. The stories hidden within its walls, the flavors of its cuisine, and the warmth of its people had captivated my heart. I was ready to uncover more of this city's secrets, knowing that with each step, Cordoba would reveal a new chapter of its captivating tale.

WELCOME TO CORDOBA

About Cordoba

Nestled in the heart of southern Spain, the city of Cordoba is a place where history whispers through narrow streets, where cultures have interwoven over centuries, and where the legacy of civilizations past stands tall as a testament to human achievement. This travel guide is your key to unlock the enchanting secrets of Cordoba, a city that continues to captivate travelers from around the world with its unique blend of Moorish, Roman, and Spanish heritage.

As we embark on this exploration, you'll discover the allure of Cordoba's geographical location, its rich historical tapestry, and its vibrant modern culture. Cordoba is not just a destination; it's a story waiting to be told.

The Geographical Marvel:

Cordoba is situated in the southern region of Spain, within the autonomous community of Andalusia. Its geographic location is nothing short of awe-inspiring. As you step foot in Cordoba, you'll find yourself on the northern banks of the mighty Guadalquivir River, one of Spain's major waterways. This river has been the lifeblood of the city, shaping its history, facilitating trade, and offering a picturesque backdrop to its urban landscape.

To the north of Cordoba, the Sierra Morena mountain range stretches, providing a stunning natural boundary. The rolling hills and lush forests of Sierra Morena offer a sharp contrast to the city's vibrant urban life, making Cordoba a place where you can experience both the tranquility of nature and the dynamism of a bustling metropolis within close proximity.

A Journey Through Time:

Cordoba's history is a mesmerizing tapestry woven from the threads of diverse cultures. The city's story dates back to Roman times when it was known as "Corduba. " Under Roman rule, Corduba flourished as an important center of trade and culture, leaving behind archaeological treasures that still peek through the city's cobblestone streets.

However, it was during the Islamic rule that Cordoba reached its zenith. The Caliphate of Cordoba, established in the 8th century, transformed the city into a beacon of learning, art, and architecture. The crowning jewel of this era is the Great Mosque of Cordoba (Mezquita-Catedral), a breathtaking testament to the architectural genius of its time. Today, this UNESCO World Heritage Site stands as a symbol of religious and cultural harmony.

With the Reconquista in the 13th century, Cordoba returned to Christian rule, ushering in yet another chapter of its rich history. Spanish Catholicism left its mark on the city, evident in the beautiful cathedrals and churches that coexist alongside Islamic architectural marvels.

As you delve deeper into the chapters of this travel guide, you'll have the privilege of exploring these historical layers, uncovering hidden gems, and tracing the footsteps of emperors, caliphs, and monarchs who once walked these very streets.

A Living Legacy

Cordoba is not merely a relic of the past; it's a living, breathing city with a vibrant culture that pays homage to its diverse heritage. The echoes of flamenco music fill the air, tapas bars beckon with tantalizing aromas, and festivals like the May Crosses Festival and the Cordoba Fair add color and fervor to daily life.

This travel guide is your compass to navigate through Cordoba's treasures, both old and new. As you flip the pages and embark on your journey through this historic city, prepare to be captivated by the timeless charm of Cordoba, where the past and present dance harmoniously, creating an unforgettable experience for every traveler. So, let's begin our exploration of this enchanting city, where history, culture, and beauty converge to create a truly unique destination. Welcome to Cordoba.

Culture and People

The culture of Cordoba is a unique blend of different influences, including Moorish, Jewish, and Christian traditions. The city is known for its vibrant arts scene, with many museums, art galleries, and theatres. The Moorish influence can be seen in the architecture of the city, with its arched doorways, intricate tilework, and beautiful gardens. The Jewish Quarter is also a popular tourist destination, with its narrow streets and beautiful synagogues. The people of Cordoba are proud of their multicultural heritage, and they are known for their hospitality and love of life.

Weather and Climate

Weather and Climate of Cordoba

Cordoba, situated in southern Spain, experiences a Mediterranean climate with some distinctive characteristics. Understanding the weather and climate in Cordoba is essential for planning your visit to this historic city. Here's an overview:

Summers (June to August)

  - Summers in Cordoba are long, hot, and dry. This is the most challenging season in terms of weather, with temperatures often soaring above

35°C (95°F) and occasionally reaching well into the 40s°C (100s°F).

- The city is known for its scorching temperatures, especially in July and August. It's advisable to stay hydrated, wear sunscreen, and seek shade during the peak of the day.

- Despite the heat, summer is the tourist high season due to the city's many festivals and events. Visitors can enjoy the vibrant atmosphere of the May Crosses Festival and the Cordoba Fair during this time.

Autumn (September to November)

- Autumn in Cordoba is a pleasant transition period. Temperatures start to cool down from the extreme heat of summer, making it a comfortable time for outdoor exploration.

- September can still be warm, but by October, the weather becomes more temperate, with daytime highs ranging from 20°C to 30°C (68°F to 86°F).

- This season offers a more relaxed atmosphere for sightseeing, and you can enjoy the changing colors of the city's gardens and courtyards.

Winters (December to February)

- Cordoba's winters are mild compared to other parts of Europe. While it rarely snows, temperatures can drop to around 5°C to 15°C (41°F to 59°F) during the day.

- Evenings and nights can get chilly, so it's advisable to bring layers and a jacket for the cooler hours.

- Winter is an excellent time for budget travelers, as accommodation prices tend to be lower than in the peak tourist season.

Spring (March to May)

- Spring is one of the most delightful times to visit Cordoba. The weather is mild and comfortable, with daytime temperatures ranging from 15°C to 25°C (59°F to 77°F).

- The city comes to life with the blooming of flowers, particularly during the May Crosses Festival when the courtyards are adorned with colorful displays.

- Spring is a popular time for tourists seeking a balance between pleasant weather and fewer crowds.

Special Note:

Cordoba is known for its siesta culture, where many businesses and shops close for a few hours in the early afternoon during the hottest months. This is a good time for tourists to relax or enjoy a leisurely lunch.

In summary, Cordoba's climate features hot, dry summers and mild, relatively wet winters. Spring and autumn offer more temperate conditions and are considered ideal for exploring the city. When planning your visit, consider the weather and your comfort, and choose a season that aligns with your preferences.

10 REASONS WHY EVERYONE SHOULD VISIT CORDOBA.

Here are ten reasons why everyone should consider visiting Cordoba

Architectural Marvel – Mezquita-Catedral

Cordoba boasts the magnificent Mezquita-Catedral, a symbol of religious harmony. This architectural wonder seamlessly blends Islamic and Christian design, leaving visitors in awe of its intricate arches and stunning beauty.

Historic Jewish Quarter

Explore the city's Jewish Quarter, a labyrinth of narrow streets, courtyards, and whitewashed buildings. This area preserves Cordoba's Jewish heritage and is a UNESCO World Heritage Site.

Romantic Courtyards (Patios) Cordoba is famous for its enchanting flower-filled courtyards. Visit during the Cordoba Patio Festival in May to witness the courtyards in their full, vibrant glory.

Flamenco Culture

Immerse yourself in the passionate world of flamenco. Cordoba is renowned for its authentic and intimate flamenco performances that captivate the soul.

Mesmerizing Gardens –

Alcázar de los Reyes Cristianos**: Stroll through the gardens of the Alcázar, the former residence of Catholic monarchs. These lush gardens offer a tranquil escape from the bustling city.

Historical Bridges

Cross the Roman Bridge, an ancient stone bridge with 16 arches, and marvel at the views of the Mezquita-Catedral and the Guadalquivir River.

Culinary Delights

Savor Cordoba's unique cuisine. Try salmorejo (a cold tomato soup), flamenquín (a fried meat dish), and a variety of tapas in local taverns.

Festivals and Celebrations

Experience the city's vibrant festivals, such as the Feria de Cordoba, a lively fair with music, dance, and traditional costumes, and Semana Santa, a dramatic Holy Week procession.

Museum Treasures

Visit the Archaeological and Ethnological Museum to uncover the region's rich history, and explore the Julio Romero de Torres Museum to admire the works of the renowned Cordoban painter.

Charming Streets and Plazas

Wander through the charming streets of Cordoba's historic center, where every turn reveals hidden squares, fountains, and charming cafes.

Cordoba is a city where the past harmonizes with the present, offering a unique blend of history, culture, and natural beauty. Each of these reasons is a testament to why Cordoba deserves a spot on every traveler's bucket list, promising an unforgettable journey into the heart of Andalusia.

10 INTERESTING FACTS YOU PROBABLY DO NOT KNOW ABOUT CORDOBA

1.The Great Mosque's Remarkable Pillars

The Great Mosque of Cordoba (Mezquita-Catedral) boasts a mesmerizing forest of over 850 columns, many of which were reclaimed from Roman and Visigothic structures. The visual effect inside the mosque is a testament to Islamic architecture's ingenuity.

2.Bridge with a History

The Roman Bridge of Cordoba, known as "Puente Romano, " has been standing for over two millennia. It was originally built in the 1st century BC and has been renovated multiple times. It provides breathtaking views of the city.

3. Floral Courtyards

Cordoba is famous for its "patios, " or courtyards, adorned with vibrant flowers. In fact, there's an annual competition called the Cordoba Patio

Festival where residents open their patios to the public, creating a riot of colors and scents.

4.The Caliphal Baths

Cordoba is home to well-preserved Caliphal Baths, remnants of a sophisticated Islamic bathing culture. These baths provide a glimpse into the opulence of medieval Cordoba.

5.The Annual May Crosses Festival

In early May, Cordoba comes alive with the "Cruces de Mayo" festival. Neighborhoods compete to create the most stunning flower-covered crosses, accompanied by music, dancing, and traditional food.

6.Birthplace of the Spanish Inquisition

Unfortunately, Cordoba also has a darker historical association as the birthplace of the Spanish Inquisition. It was founded here in the 13th century to investigate and punish religious non-conformity.

7.Cordoban Cuisine

Cordoban cuisine is a blend of influences, including Moorish, Jewish, and Christian. Try traditional dishes like salmorejo (a cold tomato soup), flamenquín (breaded and fried ham or chicken), and various tapas.

8.Hidden Courtyards

While exploring Cordoba's old town, keep an eye out for hidden courtyards and squares. They often lead to unexpected discoveries, like charming cafes or artisan workshops.

9. Roman Mausoleum Tower

Near the city's historic center, you'll find the Roman Mausoleum Tower, a well-preserved burial site dating back to the 1st century AD. It's a fascinating glimpse into Cordoba's Roman past.

10.Famous Residents

Cordoba has been home to several notable figures, including the philosopher Seneca, the Jewish philosopher Maimonides, and the Roman poet Lucan.

These intriguing facts showcase the diverse and rich history, culture, and traditions of Cordoba.

VISA REQUIREMENTS FOR CORDOBA

For travelers embarking on a journey to the captivating city of Cordoba, one of the essential considerations is understanding the visa requirements for entry into Spain, specifically Cordoba. This chapter serves as your guide to navigating the sometimes complex world of visas and permits, ensuring that your travel plans to Cordoba unfold seamlessly.

Visa Basics:

Before diving into the specifics of visa requirements, it's crucial to grasp the fundamental concept of visas. A visa is a document that grants a foreign national permission to enter, stay, and travel within a specific country or region for a designated period. In the context of Cordoba, you will be traveling to Spain, and therefore, you'll need to understand Spain's visa regulations.

Schengen Area:

Cordoba, like the rest of Spain, falls within the Schengen Area, an agreement among European countries to abolish internal borders and allow for seamless travel within the region. This means that the type of visa you need to enter Cordoba often depends on your nationality and the purpose of your visit.

Visa Exemptions:

It's important to note that citizens of many countries enjoy visa exemptions when visiting the Schengen Area, including Spain, for short stays (typically up to 90 days within a 180-day period). These exemptions are primarily for tourists, business travelers, and those visiting family and friends. However, the specific list of exempt countries can change, so it's essential to verify your eligibility before planning your trip.

Tourist Visas:

If you are not eligible for a visa exemption, or if your intended stay exceeds 90 days, you will need to apply for a Schengen Tourist Visa through the Spanish consulate or embassy in your home country. This visa is designed for individuals who plan to visit Cordoba and other destinations in Spain

for tourism purposes. You will need to provide various documents, including proof of accommodation, travel itinerary, travel insurance, and sufficient financial means to cover your stay.
Student and Work Visas:

For those planning to study or work in Cordoba, a different type of visa may be required. Student visas are typically issued for the duration of your academic program, while work visas are granted when you have secured a job offer in Spain. Each of these visa categories has its own specific requirements and application processes, so it's advisable to consult the Spanish consulate or embassy in your home country for detailed guidance.
Residence Permits:

If you intend to live in Cordoba for an extended period, such as for retirement, family reunification, or other non-tourist reasons, you may need to apply for a residence permit. These permits are subject to Spanish immigration laws and can be complex, often requiring proof of financial stability, healthcare coverage, and other supporting documentation.

Plan Ahead:

Understanding the visa requirements for Cordoba and Spain is a crucial step in your travel planning process. It's advisable to begin the visa application process well in advance of your intended travel dates, as processing times can vary, and appointments at consulates or embassies may be limited.

we've provided an overview of the visa landscape for Cordoba, but remember that visa regulations can change, so it's essential to consult the official website of the Spanish consulate or embassy in your home country for the most up-to-date and accurate information. Ensuring that your visa matters are in order will allow you to focus on the excitement and wonder that await you in the beautiful city of Cordoba..

THE BEST TIME TO VISIT CORDOBA

As you embark on your journey through this comprehensive Cordoba travel guide, it's crucial to consider the timing of your visit. Cordoba, like many destinations, experiences distinct seasons and weather patterns throughout the year. The best time to visit Cordoba largely depends on your preferences, whether you seek pleasant weather, vibrant festivals, or quieter moments to explore its historical treasures.

The Golden Seasons: Spring and Autumn

For travelers who relish temperate weather and fewer crowds, spring (March to May) and autumn (September to November) are the golden seasons to explore Cordoba. During these months, the city enjoys mild temperatures, making it ideal for walking tours, outdoor exploration, and al fresco dining. The blooming flowers and blossoming orange trees add a touch of natural beauty to Cordoba's historic streets.

In spring, Cordoba comes alive with the scent of flowers during the renowned Patios Festival (Festival de los Patios) held in May. This festival showcases the city's hidden courtyard gardens, adorned with vibrant blooms. It's a unique opportunity to experience Cordoba's local culture and witness the creativity of its residents.

Summer: Vibrancy and Festivals

Summer (June to August) is undoubtedly the busiest time in Cordoba, as tourists flock to the city to bask in the sun and partake in its lively atmosphere. However, be prepared for scorching temperatures, especially in July and August, when daytime highs can soar well above 90°F (32°C). Despite the heat, summer in Cordoba offers a unique charm.

One of the highlights of summer is the Cordoba Fair (Feria de Córdoba), typically held in late May to early June. This vibrant festival features flamenco music, traditional food, and colorful casetas (tents) where locals and visitors gather to celebrate. It's an exhilarating experience, but booking accommodations well in advance is advisable.

Autumn: Tranquility and Cultural Delights

As summer fades into autumn, Cordoba regains its tranquility, making it a delightful time to explore the city's historical sites without the hustle and bustle of peak tourist season. The weather remains pleasant, and you'll have the opportunity to enjoy cultural events, such as the Guitar Festival (Festival de la Guitarra) in July and the International Sephardic Music Festival (Festival Internacional de Música Sefardí) in September.

Winter: A Quiet Retreat

If you prefer solitude and wish to immerse yourself in the serenity of Cordoba's historical treasures, winter (December to February) may be the right time for you. While temperatures can be cooler, ranging from 45°F to 60°F (7°C to 15°C), Cordoba experiences fewer tourists during this season. You'll have the unique opportunity to explore the Mezquita-Catedral and other attractions without the crowds, providing a more intimate experience.

Winter in Cordoba is also a time to savor hearty Andalusian cuisine, warm up with a glass of local wine, and engage with the friendly locals who are always eager to share their city's rich history.

In this travel guide, we've explored the best times to visit Cordoba, each offering its own set of experiences. The choice is yours, guided by your preferences for weather, crowd levels, and the unique festivals that add vibrancy to this remarkable city. Whether you seek the vibrancy of summer or the tranquility of winter, Cordoba promises to enchant you with its timeless charm and cultural treasures.

GETTING TO CORDOBA

Cordoba, with its rich history and cultural treasures, is a city that beckons travelers from around the world. Getting to this enchanting destination is relatively straightforward, thanks to its strategic location in southern Spain. In this section, we'll explore the various modes of transportation available to travelers seeking to reach Cordoba.

By Air:

For international travelers, the most common way to reach Cordoba is by flying into the Adolfo Suárez Madrid-Barajas Airport (MAD) or the Seville Airport (SVQ). Both airports are well-connected to major international destinations and offer various flight options.

From Madrid-Barajas Airport:
- Cordoba is approximately 400 kilometers (about 250 miles) southwest of Madrid.

- You can choose to take a domestic flight from Madrid to Cordoba's Airport (Aeropuerto de Córdoba, ODB), which offers several daily connections.

- Alternatively, you can take a high-speed train or a bus from Madrid to Cordoba, as explained in the sections below.

From Seville Airport:

- Cordoba is approximately 140 kilometers (about 87 miles) northeast of Seville.

- You can take a domestic flight from Seville to Cordoba's Airport (ODB) or opt for train or bus travel.

By Train:

Cordoba boasts excellent rail connectivity, making it easily accessible by train. The Cordoba Central Railway Station (Estación de Córdoba-Central) is a major transportation hub in the city, well-served by both domestic and international train services.

AVE High-Speed Train: Renfe's AVE high-speed train network connects Cordoba to major Spanish cities like Madrid (approximately 1. 5-2 hours journey), Seville (approximately 40-50 minutes journey), and Barcelona (approximately 4. 5 hours journey). These high-speed trains offer a comfortable and efficient way to reach Cordoba.

Regional Trains: If you're traveling from nearby towns or cities within Andalusia, regional trains are available. These may take a bit longer but offer a cost-effective option. By Bus:

Traveling to Cordoba by bus is another viable option, especially if you're looking for a budget-friendly journey. The Cordoba Bus Station (Estación de Autobuses) is conveniently located in the city center.

National and International Buses**: Several bus companies operate services connecting Cordoba to various Spanish cities, including Madrid, Seville, Granada, and more. Additionally, there are international bus services to neighboring countries like Portugal.

By Car:

If you prefer the flexibility of driving, you can rent a car and reach Cordoba via Spain's well-maintained road network. The city is accessible by major highways, including the A-4, which connects Cordoba to Madrid and Seville.

Please keep in mind that driving in the city center may be challenging due to narrow streets and limited parking options. It's advisable to check the parking facilities at your accommodation in advance if you plan to travel by car.

In conclusion, Cordoba is well-connected by air, train, and bus services, making it accessible to travelers from various destinations. Whether you choose the convenience of flying, the speed of high-speed trains, or the scenic route of a bus journey, Cordoba eagerly awaits your arrival to share its captivating history and culture.

SOME DO'S AND DON'TS FOR PEOPLE VISITING CORDOBA.

Do's

Respect Cultural Differences: Embrace the rich cultural diversity of Cordoba. Show respect for local customs, traditions, and religious practices, especially when visiting places of worship like the Great Mosque.

2.Learn Basic Spanish Phrases:

While many locals may speak English, making an effort to communicate in Spanish, even if it's just a few basic phrases, can go a long way in building positive interactions.

3.Visit the Great Mosque (Mezquita-Catedral):

This iconic monument is a must-visit. Explore its stunning architecture, including the mesmerizing forest of columns and the Christian cathedral built within. Remember to dress modestly when visiting.

4.Indulge in Tapas:

Cordoba is known for its delicious tapas. Do try the local dishes at tapas bars and experience the authentic flavors of Andalusian cuisine.

5.Stroll Through the Jewish Quarter (Judería):
Explore the historic Jewish Quarter's narrow streets, white-washed buildings, and picturesque patios. It's a great place for leisurely walks and discovering hidden gems.

6.Experience Flamenco:
Attend a live Flamenco performance to immerse yourself in this passionate and iconic Spanish art form. Cordoba offers some excellent venues for Flamenco shows.

7. Stay Hydrated:
Cordoba can get quite hot, especially in the summer. Carry a water bottle with you and stay hydrated throughout the day.

8. Use Public Transportation: Utilize the city's efficient public transportation system, including

buses and trams, to get around. It's cost-effective and eco-friendly.

9. Plan for Siesta Time:

 Keep in mind that many shops and businesses may close for a siesta break during the afternoon, typically between 2:00 PM and 5:00 PM. Plan your activities accordingly.

Don'ts

1.Don't underestimate the weather: Don't Forget Sun Protection:** The sun in Cordoba can be intense, especially in the summer. Don't forget to wear sunscreen, sunglasses, and a hat to protect yourself from the sun's rays.

2.Don't Over-Tip:

Tipping is appreciated but not obligatory in Spain. A small tip (around 10%) is customary in restaurants, but check your bill, as some places may include a service charge.

3.Don't Dress Inappropriately

When visiting religious sites like the Great Mosque, avoid wearing revealing or beachwear-style clothing. Dress modestly and respectfully.

4. Don't Assume Everyone Speaks English:

While Cordoba is a tourist-friendly city, not everyone you encounter may speak English fluently. Having a translation app or phrasebook can be helpful.

5. Don't Disrupt Siesta:

During siesta hours, avoid making loud noises or engaging in activities that could disturb the peace and quiet of residential areas.

6.Don't Ignore Local Advice:

Pay attention to local recommendations regarding water consumption, especially in the summer heat. Dehydration can be a concern.

7.Don't Leave Litter:

Keep the city clean by disposing of your trash in designated bins. Avoid leaving litter in public spaces.

8.Don't Bargain Aggressively:

Bargaining is not a common practice in most shops and markets in Cordoba. Save haggling for situations where it's explicitly encouraged, like at some souvenir stalls.

By following these do's and don'ts, travelers can make the most of their visit to Cordoba while respecting local customs and ensuring a positive and memorable experience in this beautiful city.

TRAVELING AROUND CORDOBA

In the heart of Andalusia, where the Guadalquivir River flows gently beneath the watchful gaze of the Sierra Morena mountains, navigating the enchanting city of Cordoba becomes a journey through time itself. In this chapter, we will be your guides, showing you the myriad ways to traverse this remarkable city, where each street corner whispers tales of centuries gone by. As you embark on your adventure in Cordoba, prepare to be captivated by the intricate network of transportation, from the historic to the modern, that facilitates exploration.

1. The Old Town - A Stroll Through History

As you step into the labyrinthine alleys of Cordoba's Old Town (Casco Antiguo), you'll find that walking is often the best way to absorb the city's rich history and architectural splendors. Cobbled streets, lined with whitewashed buildings adorned with colorful flowerpots, beckon you to wander at your own pace.

2. Cordoba on Two Wheels - Bicycles

For the eco-conscious traveler, Cordoba offers a network of bike lanes and rental services that provide an exciting and sustainable way to explore the city. The gentle terrain and the pleasant climate make cycling an enjoyable mode of transportation. You can pedal your way through the charming streets, reaching iconic landmarks such as the Great Mosque of Cordoba with ease.

3. Horse-Drawn Carriages - Timeless Elegance

To experience Cordoba with a touch of elegance and a nod to its historical roots, consider taking a horse-drawn carriage ride. These carriages are a romantic and unique way to see the city, offering a leisurely journey through its picturesque streets. They often depart from the historic Mezquita-Catedral area and provide an enchanting perspective of Cordoba's beauty.

4. Public Transportation - Buses and Trams

Cordoba boasts an efficient and affordable public transportation system, making it convenient to travel around the city. Buses and trams crisscross Cordoba, connecting the Old Town with modern districts and suburbs. You can purchase single tickets or cost-effective travel cards for multiple journeys.

5. Taxis - Door-to-Door Convenience

Taxis are readily available in Cordoba and are a convenient option for travelers who prefer direct transportation. While they are more expensive than public transportation, they offer a comfortable and efficient way to reach specific destinations or return to your accommodation after a day of exploration.

6. Cordoba by Car - Freedom to Explore

If you plan to venture beyond the city limits to explore the surrounding Andalusian countryside or nearby attractions, renting a car can provide the flexibility you need. Just be prepared for the narrow, winding streets of the Old Town, which may not be suitable for larger vehicles.

7. Guided Tours - Expert Insights

Consider joining guided tours to gain deeper insights into Cordoba's history and culture. Knowledgeable guides can lead you through the city's iconic landmarks and hidden gems, offering historical context and fascinating stories along the way.

As you embark on your journey through Cordoba, remember that each mode of transportation offers a unique perspective on the city's diverse tapestry. Whether you choose to meander on foot, pedal along the bike lanes, or embrace the elegance of a horse-drawn carriage, you'll find that every method of travel in Cordoba is a doorway to discovery. So, as you turn the page and continue your exploration, be prepared to be transported not just through physical space but also through time and culture, as Cordoba unfolds its treasures before your eyes.

COST OF A TRIP TO CORDOBA

While the exact cost can vary depending on individual preferences and circumstances, you can provide a general breakdown of expenses to help travelers plan their budgets effectively. Here's a rough estimate of the cost of a trip to Cordoba:

1. Accommodation

  - Budget Travel: €30-€60 per night for hostels or budget hotels.

  - Mid-Range Travel: €80-€150 per night for three-star to four-star hotels.

  - Luxury Travel: €200+ per night for five-star hotels or boutique accommodations.

2.Food and Dining:

  - Budget Travel: €10-€20 per meal at local restaurants and tapas bars.

  - Mid-Range Travel: €25-€50 per meal at mid-range restaurants.

  - Luxury Travel: €100+ per meal at upscale restaurants.

3. Transportation:

- Local Transportation: €1. 30 per bus/tram ride or €10 for a multi-day pass.

- Taxis: Starting fare of around €3. 50, with additional charges per kilometer.

- High-Speed Train (e. G. , Madrid to Cordoba): €40-€100+ one-way, depending on class and booking time.

4. Attractions and Activities:

- Entrance to Mezquita-Catedral: €10-€15 (as of my last knowledge update in September 2021).

- Other Attractions: Budget around €5-€10 per attraction.

- Guided Tours: Prices vary; consider group tours for cost savings.

5. Shopping and Souvenirs:

Budget according to personal shopping preferences.

6. Miscellaneous Expenses:

- Travel Insurance: Varies based on coverage and duration of the trip.

- Mobile Data and SIM Cards: €10-€30 for a local SIM card with data.

- Tips and Gratuities: Typically 10% of the bill at restaurants.

7. Flights:

The cost of airfare to Cordoba will vary widely depending on your departure location, airline choice, and booking time. Be sure to check for deals and discounts.

8. Travel Extras:

Consider additional expenses for optional activities, spa treatments, or special experiences.

It's important to note that these estimates are approximate and can fluctuate based on factors like the time of year you visit, currency exchange rates, and personal spending habits. Encourage readers to research and plan their trip budgets carefully, taking into account any special discounts, promotions, or travel packages that may be available during their visit.

Additionally, remind travelers to always have some extra funds set aside for emergencies or unexpected expenses. By providing this cost breakdown, your readers will have a practical starting point for planning their trip to Cordoba and can adjust their budget based on their unique preferences and circumstances.

TRAVEL TIPS TO SAVE MONEY

1. Plan Ahead:

   - Begin your journey by planning well in advance. Booking flights, accommodations, and activities ahead of time can often result in significant cost savings.

2. Travel During Off-Peak Seasons:

   - Consider visiting Cordoba during its off-peak seasons. This not only means fewer crowds but also lower prices for accommodations and attractions.

3. Accommodation Options:

   - Explore a range of accommodation options, from budget-friendly hostels to boutique hotels. You can often find charming and affordable lodgings in the heart of Cordoba.

4. Public Transportation:

   - Utilize Cordoba's efficient public transportation system, including buses and trams, to get around the city economically. Consider purchasing multi-day transport passes for added savings.

5. Free and Low-Cost Attractions:

- Take advantage of the many free or low-cost attractions in Cordoba, such as exploring the historic Old Town, strolling along the Roman Bridge, and visiting local markets.

6. Tapas Culture:

- Embrace the Spanish tapas culture. Many bars offer complimentary tapas with your drinks, making it an affordable way to sample local cuisine.

7. Lunchtime Menus:

- Opt for the "menu del día" at local restaurants during lunchtime. These fixed-price menus offer a great value for a multi-course meal.

8. Student and Senior Discounts:

- If eligible, don't forget to ask for student or senior discounts at museums, theaters, and attractions. Your ID card might save you money.

9. Water and Snacks:

- Carry a reusable water bottle to refill from fountains and choose local markets for affordable snacks instead of relying on expensive tourist spots.

10. Language Skills:

- Learn a few basic Spanish phrases. Locals appreciate the effort, and it can help with bargaining and navigating the city's streets.

11. Travel Insurance:

- While it may seem like an added expense, having travel insurance can save you money in case of unexpected situations like medical emergencies or trip cancellations.

12. Budgeting Apps:

- Download budgeting apps to track your spending during your trip. This helps you stay within your budget and identify areas where you can cut costs.

13. Souvenir Shopping:

- Be selective with souvenirs. Look for locally made or unique products that are often more affordable and meaningful than generic tourist items.

14. Walk and Explore:

- Cordoba's Old Town is best explored on foot. Walking not only allows you to experience the city intimately but also saves money on transportation.

15. Guided Tours:

- Consider free or low-cost guided walking tours to gain insights into the city's history and culture. It's an economical way to learn about Cordoba.

16. Plan Your Dining Outings:

- Choose a few special restaurants for dining out, but also enjoy affordable local eateries for most of your meals. This balance keeps your budget in check.

By incorporating these money-saving travel tips into your Cordoba travel guide, you'll provide valuable insights to travelers looking to explore this beautiful city without breaking the bank. These tips not only help visitors save money but also enable them to experience Cordoba's culture and history to the fullest.

THINGS TO BRING ON A TRIP

here's a list of essential items to bring on your trip to Cordoba,

1. Travel Documents:

  - Passport and visa (if required).

  - Photocopies of important documents, stored separately.

  - Travel insurance information.

  - Itinerary with hotel reservations and contact details.

2. Money and Payment Methods:

  - Local currency (Euros) and some small bills for tips.

  - Credit/debit cards with international capabilities.

  - A money belt or secure wallet for keeping valuables safe.

3. Clothing:

  - Comfortable walking shoes for exploring the city.

- Lightweight, breathable clothing for the warm Andalusian weather.

- A light jacket or shawl for cooler evenings.

- Swimwear if you plan to visit pools or nearby beaches.

4. Electronics:

- Smartphone and charger with a travel adapter.

- Power bank for recharging on the go.

- Camera or smartphone for capturing memories.

- Headphones for entertainment during transit.

5. Travel Essentials:

- Travel-sized toiletries, including sunscreen and insect repellent.

- Prescription medications, if applicable, along with a copy of prescriptions.

- Travel-sized first aid kit with essentials like band-aids and pain relievers.

- Travel pillow and eye mask for comfortable rest during long journeys.

6. Travel Accessories:

- Travel guidebook or map of Cordoba.

- Language phrasebook or translation app for basic Spanish.

- Travel backpack or daypack for carrying essentials during city exploration.

- Reusable water bottle to stay hydrated.

- Ziplock bags for storing snacks or small items.

- Travel locks and cable ties for added security.

7. Entertainment and Comfort:

- Books, e-readers, or magazines for leisure reading.

- Travel-sized umbrella or rain jacket, especially if visiting during the rainy season.

- Travel-sized laundry detergent if you plan on doing laundry.

- Adapters for electronics to ensure they can be charged.

8. Miscellaneous:

- Sunglasses and a hat to protect against the sun.

- Travel-sized sewing kit for minor repairs.

- Travel-friendly stain remover pen.

- Travel journal or notepad for jotting down memories and notes.

- Any specific items you require, such as specialized gear for outdoor activities.

9. Eco-Friendly Choices:
- Reusable shopping bag to reduce plastic waste.
- Eco-friendly toiletries to minimize environmental impact.
- Refillable travel-sized containers for toiletries.

Remember that Cordoba can get quite hot in the summer, so it's essential to stay hydrated and wear sunscreen. Additionally, the city has a rich cultural and historical heritage, so don't forget your curiosity and enthusiasm for exploring the many wonders that await you. Your journey to Cordoba promises to be an enriching and unforgettable experience. luggage.

10 TOP ATTRACTIONS YOU SHOULD SEE WHEN YOU VISIT CORDOBA

Here are some of the top attractions to see in Cordoba

The Great Mosque of Cordoba

The Great Mosque of Cordoba, also known as the Mezquita-Catedral, is one of the most extraordinary and historically significant architectural wonders in Spain. Here's a detailed explanation:

Historical Significance:

The Great Mosque of Cordoba holds a unique place in history. Its construction began in 785 AD when Cordoba was the capital of the Umayyad Caliphate in Spain. Over the centuries, it went through various expansions and modifications, reflecting the region's diverse rulers, including Muslims, Christians, and Jews. It stands as a symbol of the religious and cultural transitions that occurred in Spain.

Architectural Marvel:

The mosque's architecture is a testament to Islamic art and engineering prowess. The structure initially featured a vast prayer hall with a mesmerizing forest of over 850 columns, each supporting double-tiered horseshoe arches. The play of light and shadow through these arches creates a breathtaking visual effect, making the interior feel like a mystical oasis.

Mihrab and Maqsura:

The mihrab, a semi-circular niche indicating the direction of Mecca, is a masterpiece of Islamic art. Its intricate mosaics and calligraphy are renowned for their precision and beauty. Nearby, the maqsura, an enclosure for the caliph, showcases the mosque's grandeur and the opulence of the Umayyad period.

The Christian Transformation:

After Cordoba was reclaimed by Christian forces in 1236, the mosque was transformed into a cathedral. The insertion of a Gothic cathedral nave into the mosque's center is a remarkable example of blending two contrasting architectural styles. The blend of Islamic and Christian elements is most evident in the Renaissance-era choir and the Baroque altar. This unique fusion has earned the structure its dual name, the Mezquita-Catedral.

Patio de los Naranjos:

Before entering the mosque-cathedral, visitors pass through the Patio de los Naranjos, a tranquil courtyard adorned with fragrant orange trees and fountains. This space provides a moment of serenity and reflection before experiencing the grandeur inside.

Visitor Experience:

Today, the Great Mosque of Cordoba is open to visitors as both a place of worship and a historical site. Tourists from around the world come to marvel at its architectural magnificence and the layers of history within its walls. It has been a UNESCO World Heritage Site since 1984, recognizing its universal cultural significance.

In conclusion, the Great Mosque of Cordoba, the Mezquita-Catedral, stands as a living testament to the ebb and flow of civilizations and religious traditions in Spain. Its awe-inspiring architecture and historical richness make it a must-visit destination for anyone interested in the intersection of art, culture, and religion.

The Alcázar de los Reyes Cristianos

The Alcázar de los Reyes Cristianos, often simply referred to as the Alcázar, is a historic fortress-palace located in Córdoba, Spain. This remarkable architectural gem is steeped in history, offering a fascinating glimpse into Spain's rich past.

Historical Significance:

The Alcázar de los Reyes Cristianos has a history that dates back to the Roman era. Initially, it served as a Roman fortress, but its true significance emerged during the Islamic rule of Spain. The Alcázar was expanded and renovated by the Umayyad Caliphate in the 8th century, becoming a royal residence and symbolizing the cultural and artistic achievements of Islamic Cordoba.

Christian Reconquest:

After the Christian Reconquest of Córdoba in the 13th century, the Alcázar underwent significant changes. It became a royal residence for Ferdinand and Isabella, the Catholic Monarchs, who used it as a base during the final stages of the Reconquista. Here, Christopher Columbus famously requested their support for his voyage to the Americas.

Architectural Marvel;

The Alcázar's architecture is a blend of Islamic, Gothic, and Renaissance styles, showcasing the diverse influences that have shaped Spain's cultural heritage. Its interior courtyards, gardens, and intricate tilework are especially noteworthy. The Alcázar is also known for its beautiful Moorish baths, which are reminiscent of the Islamic influence on the building.

Gardens and Courtyards:

The Alcázar's gardens are a tranquil oasis within the fortress. They include lush greenery, reflecting pools, and fountains. The gardens are divided into four main sections, each with its own unique character, such as the famous "Patio de los Naranjos" (Courtyard of the Orange Trees) and the "Patio de los Reyes" (Courtyard of the Kings).

Inquisition and Preservation:
During the Spanish Inquisition, the Alcázar was used as a prison, and it witnessed many dark chapters in Spanish history. However, it was later restored and preserved as a national monument.

Visiting Today:
Today, the Alcázar de los Reyes Cristianos is open to the public, allowing visitors to explore its rich history, architecture, and beautifully landscaped gardens. It Is a UNESCO World Heritage Site and one of Córdoba's most iconic landmarks.

Visiting the Alcázar is like stepping back in time and immersing yourself in the layers of history that have shaped Spain. It's a must-see destination for history enthusiasts, architecture aficionados, and anyone seeking to understand the cultural tapestry of this beautiful country.

The Jewish Quarter

The Jewish Quarter, or "Judería" in Spanish, is a fascinating and historically rich neighborhood found in many Spanish cities, including Salamanca. Let's explore the depth and significance of Salamanca's Jewish Quarter:

Historical Significance:
Salamanca's Jewish Quarter is a testament to the city's multicultural past. During the Middle Ages, a thriving Jewish community lived here, contributing significantly to the city's intellectual and cultural development. They coexisted with Christian and Muslim communities, creating a vibrant, diverse atmosphere.

Architecture and Layout:
As you wander through Salamanca's Jewish Quarter, you'll notice the distinct architectural features. Narrow winding streets, whitewashed

buildings with wrought-iron balconies, and charming courtyards characterize this historic area. The layout of the quarter often reflects the defensive measures taken by the Jewish community during times of persecution.

Synagogue of Salamanca:

One of the highlights of Salamanca's Jewish Quarter is the former synagogue, which is now known as the "Convento de Santa Eulalia de los Convertidos. " This building is a remarkable piece of history, reflecting the transition of Jewish places of worship to Christian use after the expulsion of Jews from Spain in 1492. Inside, you can observe elements of both Jewish and Christian architecture.

Cultural Legacy:

The Jewish community in Salamanca made significant contributions to education, philosophy, and science during the Middle Ages. They played a crucial role in translating Greek and Arabic works into Latin, which had a profound impact on European intellectual development. Their legacy is felt throughout the city's historic university and libraries.

Influence on the City:
Salamanca's Jewish Quarter serves as a reminder of the city's multicultural heritage. The coexistence of different religious and cultural groups left an indelible mark on Salamanca's identity. The Spanish Inquisition and subsequent expulsions profoundly affected the Jewish community, but their legacy persists through the neighborhood's historic sites. Preservation and Tourism:
Today, Salamanca's Jewish Quarter is a popular destination for tourists interested in exploring its history and culture. Many of the old Jewish houses have been restored and converted into shops, restaurants, and museums, offering visitors a glimpse into the past.

In conclusion, Salamanca's Jewish Quarter is a captivating blend of history, architecture, and cultural heritage. It serves as a reminder of the city's multicultural past and the enduring legacy of the Jewish community. Exploring this neighborhood allows you to step back in time and appreciate the rich tapestry of Salamanca's history.

Roman Bridge (Puente Romano)

Roman Bridge (Puente Romano) of Cordoba: A Journey Through Time

As you stand at the edge of the Guadalquivir River in Cordoba, gazing upon the architectural marvel known as the Roman Bridge (Puente Romano), you are not merely looking at a structure of stone and mortar. You are peering into the depths of history, tracing the footsteps of generations long gone, and connecting with an ancient legacy that has endured for over two millennia.

The Origins:

The Roman Bridge, an emblematic icon of Cordoba, stands as a testament to the city's rich history. It is said that the Romans, with their unparalleled engineering prowess, constructed this bridge during the 1st century BC. The purpose was simple yet monumental: to link the bustling city of Corduba (as it was known then) to the rest of the

Roman Empire. This bridge became a vital part of the Via Augusta, the Roman road that connected Cadiz in the south to Rome in the north, and its strategic location on the Guadalquivir River made it a linchpin of commerce and communication.

The Architecture:

The Roman Bridge is a breathtaking display of Roman ingenuity and precision. Its construction is a testament to the enduring craftsmanship of the Romans. The bridge, made of large stone blocks and spans over 200 meters in length, is an incredible feat of engineering. As you walk across its surface, you'll notice the rhythmic repetition of semi-circular arches, elegantly supported by sturdy piers. These arches not only provided stability but also allowed the bridge to gracefully accommodate the fluctuating waters of the Guadalquivir River.

A Witness to History:

The Roman Bridge has borne witness to the ebb and flow of history, serving as a silent spectator of

Cordoba's transformation from Roman settlement to Islamic stronghold and, eventually, to a Christian city. With the arrival of the Moors in the 8th century, the bridge was given a face-lift, as it often happened with Roman structures. They added their own unique character, with decorative alcoves and a more Islamic aesthetic.

Modern-Day Magic:

Today, the Roman Bridge remains as a living testament to Cordoba's rich past. It is no longer a bustling trade route, but it serves as a picturesque pedestrian bridge that connects the historic center of Cordoba to the Calahorra Tower on the opposite bank. As you stroll across the bridge, with the river gently flowing below and the city's historic skyline unfolding before you, you can't help but feel the weight of history in every stone.

Illuminating Nights:

The Roman Bridge takes on an entirely different character at night when its arches are beautifully illuminated, casting enchanting reflections in the river. It's a popular spot for romantic evening walks and provides a stunning backdrop for photos.

Visiting the Roman Bridge of Cordoba is not just a sightseeing experience; it's a journey through the annals of time, an opportunity to connect with the enduring spirit of a city that has evolved while cherishing its past. As you include the Roman Bridge in your Cordoba travel guide, remember that this historic icon is more than a bridge; it's a time machine that transports you through the ages and allows you to touch the soul of Cordoba's remarkable history.

Calahorra Tower (Torre de la Calahorra)

Calahorra Tower (Torre de la Calahorra): An Immortal Sentinel of Cordoba's Past

In the heart of Cordoba, nestled beside the tranquil waters of the Guadalquivir River, stands a monument to time itself—the Calahorra Tower, or "Torre de la Calahorra. " This enduring sentinel of history tells a tale that spans the centuries, whispering secrets of empires and the relentless passage of time.

A Glimpse into the Past:

The Calahorra Tower is an architectural treasure steeped in the lore of Cordoba's diverse cultural legacy. Its origins trace back to the late 12th century during the era of Al-Andalus, when Cordoba was a flourishing center of Islamic civilization. Constructed by order of the Almoravid Dynasty, it was designed as a defensive fortress at the entrance of the city.

The tower's name, "Calahorra, " derives from the Arabic "Qal'at Hurr" or "Fortress of Freedom. " It served as a guardian of the city, protecting its residents and its rich cultural heritage from external threats.

Design and Architecture:

The Calahorra Tower is an architectural masterpiece, an epitome of Al-Andalus Islamic design, and a testament to the skilled craftsmanship of the era. As you approach the tower, you are greeted by its imposing façade, which marries elements of Islamic, Moorish, and Christian architecture—a visual testament to Cordoba's rich history of conquests and cultural intermingling.

One cannot help but be captivated by the tower's sturdy walls, square-shaped base, and distinct horseshoe arches, which are quintessential features of Islamic architecture. The tower's intricate details, such as stucco work and ceramic tile mosaics, transport visitors back to the time of its construction.

The Museum of Al-Andalus Life:

Today, the Calahorra Tower serves a new purpose—one that bridges the past and the present, offering visitors a unique window into the history of Cordoba and Al-Andalus. Inside the tower, you'll find the Museum of Al-Andalus Life, a captivating journey through the annals of Cordoba's Islamic heritage.

As you explore the museum, you'll encounter a rich tapestry of exhibits showcasing various aspects of daily life during the Islamic rule, from art and architecture to science and culture. The museum's immersive displays include reconstructions of ancient Cordoban homes, providing a vivid depiction of the era's domestic life.

A Bridge Between Cultures:

The Calahorra Tower, with its layers of history, stands as a symbol of Cordoba's unique position as a crossroads of civilizations. It's a place where Islamic, Moorish, and Christian influences melded, creating a melting pot of cultures that has left an indelible mark on the city's character.

As you stand within the shadow of the Calahorra Tower, you'll be transported through time, and the echoes of bygone eras will resonate in your mind. It's a place where you can reflect on the enduring spirit of Cordoba, a city that has evolved and embraced its diverse heritage while preserving its historical treasures.

Visiting the Calahorra Tower:

When you visit Cordoba, your journey is incomplete without a pilgrimage to the Calahorra Tower. Its graceful silhouette against the Cordoban skyline beckons to travelers, inviting them to uncover the secrets of a bygone era. The museum within its walls is a time capsule, offering a glimpse into the daily life of Cordoba's residents during the heights of Al-Andalus.

As the Calahorra Tower stands with unwavering dignity, it reminds us that, in the passage of time, Cordoba's essence remains steadfast—a testament to the rich amalgamation of cultures that has shaped this extraordinary city. The Calahorra Tower, with all its beauty and historical significance, is a must-see attraction in Cordoba—a place where the past and present converge in harmonious resonance.

The Great Siege Tunnels

Palacio de Viana: Unveiling the Enigmatic Beauty of Cordoba

Nestled within Cordoba's fabled Jewish Quarter, the Palacio de Viana reveals itself as an enigmatic jewel amidst the city's rich historical tapestry. Often referred to as the "Courtyards Palace" or the "Palace of the Patios, " this 14th-century mansion beckons travelers into a world where the lines between history, architecture, and nature blur, creating an awe-inspiring symphony of beauty and tranquility.

Tracing the Heritage:

The Palacio de Viana carries echoes of a bygone era. It was originally commissioned as the residence of the Marquises of Viana, a noble lineage that has imprinted its legacy upon this palace across the ages. Step through its imposing entryway, and you are instantly transported to a time when Cordoba was a hotbed of cultural exchange and artistic brilliance.

A Masterpiece of Courtyards:

What truly sets the Palacio de Viana apart from the crowd is its remarkable assembly of 12 courtyards, each one an entity of allure and charm. These courtyards, or patios, are festooned with an astonishing array of flora, cascading water features, and architectural wonders. They embody the essence of the Andalusian courtyard tradition where form and function meld seamlessly.

Strolling through the patios is akin to embarking on a botanical odyssey. Each courtyard is a distinct work of art, from the symmetrical elegance of the Renaissance Patio to the ethereal grace of the Gothic Patio. Some greet you with the scent of citrus blossoms, others beckon with placid reflection pools, and a few unveil intricately adorned tilework that narrates the artistic magnificence of its era.

Architectural Marvel:

Beyond its entrancing courtyards, the Palacio de Viana reveals architectural splendors that mirror the tastes of different epochs. The palace showcases an intriguing fusion of Gothic, Mudejar, Renaissance, and Baroque influences. Well-preserved interiors allow visitors to trace the evolution of architectural styles across the centuries.

A highlight of the palace is the grand noble hall, an exalted chamber adorned with frescoes and stucco embellishments. The palace also cradles an impressive collection of fine art, antique furnishings, and historical relics, providing a window into the lives of the aristocratic families that once called this palace their abode.

Cultural Legacy:

The Palacio de Viana, beyond its architectural and horticultural allure, resonates with profound cultural significance. It plays a pivotal role in Cordoba's cultural fabric, participating annually in the Cordoba Patio Festival (Festival de los Patios). During this cherished tradition, residents fling open their courtyard gates, extending a warm invitation to discover the secret gardens hidden within the city.

The Experience of Palacio de Viana:

A journey to the Palacio de Viana is not merely a step back in time; it is an escape into a realm of serenity and splendor. It immerses you in the art, culture, and history of Cordoba, a retreat from the bustling thoroughfares of the city center. The palace's serenity stands in stark contrast to the vivacity of Cordoba, offering travelers a distinctive and immersive encounter that should not be omitted from their Cordoba visit.

The Palacio de Viana is Cordoba's enigma, a testament to the city's enduring allure, welcoming travelers to an exclusive encounter that unveils the harmonious coexistence of history, culture, and nature.

Cordoba Botanical Gardens (Jardín Botánico)

Cordoba Botanical Gardens (Jardín Botánico): A Verdant Sanctuary in the Heart of Cordoba

Tucked away in the midst of Cordoba's historic tapestry and lively thoroughfares, a serene sanctuary emerges to captivate the traveler's imagination—the Cordoba Botanical Gardens (Jardín Botánico). As we journey deep into the heart of Cordoba in this travel guide, we uncover a hidden treasure where the lush greenery, vibrant botanical specimens, and a captivating history coalesce into an enchanting narrative.

A Verdant Oasis Amidst History:

Cordoba stands as a testament to centuries of Roman, Moorish, and Christian influences, entwined within its very streets. Amidst this beguiling tale, the Cordoba Botanical Gardens emerges as a tranquil ode to the city's profound connection with nature. Nestled alongside the Guadalquivir River, neighboring the Alcázar de los Reyes Cristianos, these gardens present a seamless fusion of historical grandeur and organic beauty.

A Botanical Sojourn:

The origins of Cordoba Botanical Gardens trace their lineage to the mid-19th century, when the site was earmarked as a botanical haven for the University of Cordoba. Today, this meticulously curated realm spans over four hectares, boasting a diverse collection of botanical specimens that promise to intrigue aficionados of botany and charm those on a casual saunter.

The Mediterranean Biome:

Cordoba's distinctive Mediterranean climate provides an idyllic canvas for these gardens, with a spotlight on Mediterranean flora. The assortment encompasses an eclectic array of botanical specimens, ranging from fragrant herbs and indigenous arboreal marvels to exotic succulents and formidable cacti. As you wander through the garden's confines, you'll be enveloped by the alluring scents of lavender and rosemary, the dappled shade of venerable olive and fig trees, and the enchanting presence of spiny pear cacti.

Thematic Paradises:

Cordoba Botanical Gardens unfurl a botanical odyssey through varying themes and regions. Your explorations will reveal thematic zones dedicated to medicinal plants, aquatic greenery, aromatic herb gardens, and more. Each precinct proffers an unparalleled sensory journey, from the soothing resonance of cascading waters in the aquatic garden to the tantalizing fragrances in the medicinal plant section.

Historical Conservatories:

Two venerable conservatories, raised in the late 19th and early 20th centuries, house a priceless collection of tropical and subtropical flora. These magnificent iron-and-glass structures, in and of themselves architectural marvels, open a portal to a foreign realm replete with towering palms, exotic orchids, and other tropical rarities. It is as if you've been spirited away to a distant rainforest within the very heart of Cordoba.

A Living Fount of Knowledge:

Beyond its role as a sanctuary of beauty, the Cordoba Botanical Gardens serves as a vibrant fount of knowledge. The gardens regularly host a plethora of workshops, exhibitions, and guided excursions, enlightening visitors on the imperative significance of botanical diversity, sustainable practices, and the artistry of horticulture.

Practical Visitor Information:

Location: The gardens' strategic location places them in close proximity to the Alcázar de los Reyes Cristianos and the city's historic core.

Operating Hours: The Cordoba Botanical Gardens typically unfold their verdant tapestry daily; however, it is judicious to confirm their current schedule before your visit.

Entrance Fees: The entry charges are typically modest, rendering this haven an inclusive attraction for visitors of all walks.

In the midst of Cordoba's architectural wonders and historical riches, the Cordoba Botanical Gardens unveils a tranquil counterpoint, beckoning you to acquaint yourself with the city's more natural aspect. As you amble through its verdurous expanses, you'll forge a deeper connection with the harmonious concurrence of Cordoba's storied history and its thriving botanical plethora. This concealed oasis is an indispensable inclusion in your Cordoba travel guide, where history, culture, and the allure of nature converge to fashion an indelible and immersive experience.

Cordoba's Plaza de la Corredera

Cordoba's Plaza de la Corredera: A Timeless Gem in the Heart of History

Nestled in the heart of Cordoba, the Plaza de la Corredera, also known simply as La Corredera, is a captivating and historically rich square that offers a glimpse into the city's diverse past. Its remarkable history, vibrant atmosphere, and architectural charm make it an essential stop for any traveler exploring the enchanting streets of Cordoba.

Historical Significance:

The origins of La Corredera date back to the 17th century when it was constructed on the site of a Roman circus. Its history is deeply intertwined with the changing fortunes of Cordoba. In its early years, it was a place for public spectacles, including bullfights and carnivals, lending the square its unique elliptical shape. Over the centuries, it evolved to witness various historical events and architectural transformations.

The square was also used as a marketplace for goods and livestock. Its name, "Corredera, " is believed to have been derived from "correr, " meaning "to run, " as this space was once used for racing horses. This vibrant history is reflected in the enduring spirit of La Corredera.

Architectural Grandeur:

La Corredera boasts an architectural style that stands in stark contrast to the typical Andalusian aesthetic of Cordoba. The surrounding buildings, constructed in the 17th century, display the influence of the Habsburg era. These structures feature symmetrical façades, wrought-iron balconies, and large arched porticos that create a harmonious and stately ambience.

One of the most prominent buildings is the Ayuntamiento (Town Hall) of Cordoba, located on the eastern side of the square. Its elegant Baroque design and striking clock tower add to the square's allure. The surrounding buildings house various cafes, restaurants, shops, and apartments, creating a dynamic atmosphere that draws locals and visitors alike.

The Pulse of Cordoba:

La Corredera is more than just an architectural gem; it is the beating heart of Cordoba's social and cultural life. The square is a popular meeting point for locals, who gather at its numerous cafes and bars to savor coffee, tapas, or a glass of fine Andalusian wine.

During the day, it's a lively space where visitors can experience the vivacious spirit of Cordoba.

Street performers, musicians, and artisans often contribute to the festive atmosphere, adding a touch of creativity and spontaneity to the square.

Special Events and Festivals:

La Corredera also serves as the backdrop for many of Cordoba's festivals and cultural events. The square comes alive with celebrations during festivals such as the Cordoba Fair and Semana Santa (Holy Week), where processions and events take place, creating an unforgettable spectacle.

Visiting Plaza de la Corredera:

When visiting Cordoba, don't miss the opportunity to experience the captivating Plaza de la Corredera. Whether you're sipping coffee at a café, admiring the historical architecture, or simply people-watching, La Corredera offers a unique blend of history, culture, and vibrant daily life that encapsulates the spirit of Cordoba. It's a must-visit destination that will leave a lasting impression on your journey through this remarkable city.

As you explore the enchanting streets of Cordoba, make sure to allocate time for this extraordinary square and uncover the stories and secrets held within its historic walls. Plaza de la Corredera is not just a place to visit; it's an experience to cherish.

Cordoba's Patios (Los Patios de Cordoba)

Cordoba's Patios (Los Patios de Cordoba): A Floral Symphony of Culture and Tradition

Amidst the cobblestone streets and historic architecture of Cordoba, there exists a tradition that is as vibrant as it is enchanting. The Patios of Cordoba, known as "Los Patios de Cordoba, " are a living testament to the city's rich cultural heritage, its reverence for nature, and a unique sense of community. These hidden oases burst into full bloom each spring, creating a captivating tapestry of colors and scents that has captivated visitors for centuries.

A Floral Time Machine:

The tradition of adorning courtyards with lush greenery and vibrant blossoms has deep roots in Cordoba's history. It's a tradition that echoes back to the time when the city was part of the Roman Empire and was later embraced and transformed by the Moors during their rule.

The Moors introduced the concept of an inner courtyard, or "patio, " as a central element of Andalusian architecture. These spaces were designed as cool, shaded retreats from the intense summer sun, often featuring fountains and water channels that provided a soothing ambiance.

Over the centuries, this tradition continued to evolve. During the Christian Reconquista, it became an expression of both aesthetic beauty and religious devotion. Patios were adorned with religious iconography, and residents would often compete to create the most captivating and ornate displays.

The Patio Festival - A Celebration of Community:

The true magic of Cordoba's Patios is unveiled during the annual Patio Festival, or "Festival de los Patios, " held every May. This event allows the public to step behind the closed doors of these private courtyards, revealing hidden gems that are otherwise inaccessible. As you explore these patios, you'll witness a cultural dance that seamlessly blends architecture, horticulture, and community spirit.

Each participating patio is a work of art in itself, meticulously maintained and adorned with a variety of flora, including geraniums, carnations, jasmine, and bougainvillea. The colors and fragrances create a sensory wonderland, with the scent of blooming flowers mingling with the sound of fountains and the coolness of the shaded courtyards.

Competition and Creativity:

The Patio Festival is also a competition, as homeowners vie for the coveted title of "Best Patio. " Judges evaluate the patios based on a range of criteria, including the diversity of plant species, overall design, and the maintenance of the courtyard. The competition fuels creativity and inspires residents to craft increasingly impressive displays year after year.

The Social Aspect:

The Patios of Cordoba are not just about flowers; they are also a celebration of community. As you wander through the courtyards, you may have the chance to meet the proud homeowners who have invested their time and energy into maintaining these living works of art. The exchange between visitors and residents during the festival is a testament to the warmth and hospitality that characterize Cordoba.

Preservation and UNESCO Recognition:

In recognition of their historical and cultural significance, the Patios of Cordoba were inscribed as a UNESCO Intangible Cultural Heritage in 2012. This acknowledgment underlines their importance in preserving a living tradition that connects Cordoba's past with its present.

A Timeless Experience:

Visiting the Patios of Cordoba is like stepping into a timeless oasis, where nature and culture harmoniously coexist. The Festival de los Patios provides an unparalleled opportunity to immerse yourself in the heart of Cordoba's traditions, offering a truly unique and enchanting experience that will remain etched in your memory long after you've left the city.

So, as you plan your journey to Cordoba, be sure to time your visit to coincide with the Patio Festival in May. It's an experience that will leave you in awe of the beauty, history, and community spirit that flourish in these secret gardens of Cordoba

Cordoba's Museum of Fine Arts (Museo de Bellas Artes):

Cordoba's Museum of Fine Arts (Museo de Bellas Artes): A Precious Repository of Spanish Art and Culture

Concealed within the heart of Cordoba, the Museum of Fine Arts (Museo de Bellas Artes) beckons as a cultural treasure trove, inviting inquisitive minds to uncover Spain's illustrious artistic heritage. This captivating museum, ensconced in the former Convent of La Merced, serves as a testament to Cordoba's unwavering commitment to the preservation and revelation of the nation's artistic accomplishments.

A Voyage Through the Mosaic of Spanish Art:

Upon crossing the museum's threshold, one embarks on a spellbinding odyssey through the labyrinthine pages of Spanish art history. The collection unfurls from the depths of the Middle Ages to the dawning of the 20th century, unfurling an intricate tapestry with a distinct emphasis on the Andalusian and Cordoban art traditions. It is a testament not only to Cordoba's artistic legacy but to its profound contributions to Spain's cultural tableau.

The Luminary Spanish Maestros:

Within the hallowed halls of the Museo de Bellas Artes, a remarkable compendium of masterpieces by celebrated Spanish painters, including works by Bartolomé Bermejo, Antonio del Castillo, and Antonio del Castillo y Saavedra, grace the walls. Their oeuvres exemplify the finesse of Spanish artistry, capturing the nuanced interplay of light and shadow, the emotional profundity of religious and mythological themes, and the enduring influence of religion and folklore on artistic expression.

The Enigma of Goya and the Realism of Velázquez:

The gallery is home to the enigmatic and compelling works of Francisco de Goya, a luminary who deftly captures the dark undercurrents of his era, encapsulating the turbulent Napoleonic Wars and the intellectual fervor of the Spanish Enlightenment. Parallelly, the iconic Diego Velázquez, renowned for his unparalleled mastery of realism, bestows portraits and scenes that transcend the canvas, breathing life into the observer's imagination. These enduring masterpieces represent their lasting eminence as two of the most influential painters in the annals of Western art.

The Cordoban Imprint:

Intertwined with the broader Spanish narrative, the Museo de Bellas Artes serves as a testament to Cordoba's inimitable cultural and artistic heritage. The creative genius of local luminaries, notably Julio Romero de Torres, renowned for his sensuous and evocative depictions that celebrate the allure of Cordoba and its women, takes center stage. These works provide a lens through which one can delve into the distinctive artistic contributions of this city.

More Than Just Canvas:

The museum's offerings extend beyond the realm of paintings. Its comprehensive collection encompasses sculptures, decorative arts, and archaeological relics. These artifacts offer a holistic perspective on the cultural and artistic evolution of Cordoba and the broader Andalusian region.

The Museum's Enchanting Setting:

Nestled within the historic Convent of La Merced, the museum's setting is, in itself, a masterpiece. The venerable architecture, serene courtyards, and ornate cloisters harmoniously frame the art on display. The Convent's storied past, from its inception in the 13th century to its transformation into a museum, mirrors the cultural metamorphosis that Cordoba has experienced throughout its history.

A visit to the Museo de Bellas Artes transcends the conventional art exhibition. It's an immersive voyage into the heart and soul of Cordoba, an opportunity to intimately connect with the city's artistic legacy—from its local artisans to the grand masters of Spain's golden age. It's a sojourn through the annals of time, where each brushstroke and chisel's caress encapsulate the very essence of a nation's creativity. It's an experience that elevates art beyond its canvas, inviting all wanderers to participate in the artistic tapestry that has intricately woven Cordoba's unique identity into the vibrant mosaic of Spanish culture.

OFF-THE-BEATEN-PATH PLACES TO VISIT IN CORDOBA.

Cordoba is not just about its famous landmarks. It's a city with hidden gems and off-the-beaten-path places that reveal its authentic charm. In this chapter of the Cordoba travel guide, we'll uncover some of the most fascinating and lesser-known places that await the curious traveler:

1. Medina Azahara:

Just a short drive from the city, you'll find the ruins of the medieval palace-city of Medina Azahara. This archaeological site offers a mesmerizing glimpse into the opulence of Andalusian Caliphate architecture. The partially reconstructed structures, with their intricate stucco work, are a testament to the city's historical significance. Walking through these ancient ruins is like stepping back in time.

2. Palacio de Orive:

Tucked away in the heart of Cordoba's historic center, this palace-turned-cultural center often escapes the notice of tourists. It features beautiful Andalusian courtyards, an art gallery, and cultural exhibitions. Palacio de Orive is an oasis of tranquility and artistry amidst the bustling city.

3. Roman Temple (Templo Romano):

Although not as famous as the Roman Bridge, the Temple of Cordoba is a well-preserved archaeological site hidden in plain sight. It's a fascinating example of Roman influence in the city, with some of its original columns still standing.

4. Royal Stables of Cordoba (Caballerizas Reales):

These historic stables are a piece of Cordoba's equestrian heritage. Visitors can witness the Andalusian horse breed up close and enjoy equestrian performances. The architecture of the stables is impressive, making it a unique and engaging attraction.

5. Casa de las Cabezas:

This charming 14th-century house features a facade adorned with carved stone heads, hence the name "House of Heads. " Inside, you'll find a small museum that delves into Cordoba's history. The house itself is a hidden architectural gem and offers a quiet retreat from the bustling streets.

6. Cristo de los Faroles:

This lesser-known monument features a statue of Christ holding lanterns, creating a captivating scene when lit at night. It's a serene spot to reflect and enjoy the ambiance, especially during the evening when the lanterns cast a warm glow.

7. Arab Baths (Baños Árabes):

Located near the Mosque-Cathedral, these ancient Arab baths are a historical relic. The atmospheric underground chambers are a remarkable example of Moorish architecture, and the site offers insights into the bathing rituals of the past.

8. Cemetery of San Rafael:

This historic cemetery, dating back to the 19th century, is a serene place to explore. It's adorned with ornate mausoleums and sculptures, making it an unexpected and contemplative attraction.

9. Puerta del Puente:

While the Roman Bridge is famous, the nearby Puerta del Puente often goes unnoticed. This ornate gate is a remnant of the city's medieval walls and is an intriguing piece of Cordoba's architectural history.

10. Alcázar of the Christian Monarchs Gardens:

Beyond the palace, the gardens of the Alcázar hide a serene world of fountains, flowerbeds, and serene walkways. These gardens offer a tranquil escape from the crowds and a perfect place for a leisurely stroll.

CULTURES AND FESTIVALS IN CORDOBA

Cordoba is a city that pulsates with a rich tapestry of cultures and festivals, where the past comes alive in a vibrant celebration of history, religion, and tradition. As we dive into this section of the Cordoba Travel Guide, let's explore the fascinating world of the city's diverse cultures and the vibrant festivals that make it truly special.

Cultural Fusion: A Legacy of Diversity

Cordoba's cultural heritage is a testament to the interplay of various civilizations that have called the city home. Over the centuries, Romans, Visigoths, Moors, and Christians have left their indelible mark on its traditions and way of life. This remarkable fusion is most evident in Cordoba's architecture, cuisine, and festivals.

1. Moorish Legacy: The Mezquita-Catedral

The Moorish influence on Cordoba is perhaps most prominently displayed in the Great Mosque of Cordoba (Mezquita-Catedral). The structure's stunning architecture, characterized by its horseshoe arches and intricate tile work, serves as a lasting reminder of the city's Islamic past. Visitors can wander through its labyrinthine interior, marveling at the beauty of its design.

2. Semana Santa (Holy Week): Christian Traditions

During the week leading up to Easter, Cordoba comes alive with processions, pageantry, and deep religious fervor. Each brotherhood, known as a cofradía, parades through the city's streets, often in traditional hooded robes, carrying elaborate religious floats. The atmosphere is both solemn and awe-inspiring, offering a window into the profound faith of the city's residents.

3. May Crosses Festival (Fiesta de los Patios)

One of Cordoba's most famous festivals, the May Crosses Festival, celebrates the arrival of spring.

Residents decorate their patios with vibrant flowers and compete for the most beautifully adorned space. Visitors are welcome to stroll through these open courtyards, enjoying the visual splendor and the sense of community.

4. Feria de Cordoba: A Glimpse of Andalusian Culture

The Feria de Cordoba is a lively celebration of Andalusian culture. Taking place in late May or early June, it features flamenco music, traditional dance, bullfighting, and an array of delicious food and drinks. The fairground is transformed into a colorful spectacle of lights, tents, and music, and the city is adorned in festive attire.

5. Cordoba Guitar Festival

This internationally renowned music festival pays homage to Cordoba's contribution to the world of music. It features performances by famous guitarists, as well as emerging talent. The festival often includes classical, flamenco, and contemporary guitar concerts, attracting music enthusiasts from around the globe.

6. Night of San Juan (Noche de San Juan)

On June 23rd, Cordobans celebrate the Night of San Juan, marking the summer solstice with bonfires, fireworks, and midnight swims in the Guadalquivir River. It's a magical evening where locals and visitors come together to enjoy the enchanting atmosphere.

7. Flamenco: The Heartbeat of Cordoba

While not a specific festival, flamenco is an integral part of Cordoba's cultural identity. Numerous venues across the city host authentic flamenco performances, allowing travelers to experience the passion and soul-stirring music and dance of Andalusia.

8. Cordoba Guitar Festival

Cordoba is the birthplace of the Spanish guitar, and the Cordoba Guitar Festival celebrates this heritage. It features concerts, workshops, and exhibitions, showcasing the beauty and artistry of this iconic instrument.

These cultural influences and festivals weave a vivid tapestry that brings Cordoba's past and present together in a dynamic display of tradition and celebration. Visitors to Cordoba have the unique opportunity to immerse themselves in a city where history and culture are not confined to museums but live on in the streets, music, and festivities. Each of these cultural experiences and festivals adds a layer of depth to the Cordoba journey, making it a truly unforgettable destination. .

A PERFECT 7-DAY ITINERARY FOR A VISIT TO CORDOBA.

In this itinerary, we've planned a perfect 7-day trip to Gibraltar, highlighting the best places to see and things to do during your stay.

Day 1: Exploring Cordoba's Historic Center

Morning (9:00 AM - 12:00 PM):

Begin your journey in Cordoba with a visit to the Great Mosque of Cordoba (Mezquita-Catedral). Arriving early ensures a tranquil experience as you wander through this architectural masterpiece, marveling at the stunning interplay of light and shadows through the forest of columns and arches.

Lunch (12:30 PM - 2:00 PM):

Satisfy your appetite with a leisurely Spanish lunch at a nearby restaurant. Order Cordoba's famous dish, "salmorejo, " a chilled tomato soup, or try "flamenquín, " a breaded and fried ham and cheese roll.

Afternoon (2:30 PM - 6:00 PM):

After lunch, make your way to the Jewish Quarter (Judería). Explore its labyrinthine streets, taking in the atmosphere of its charming squares and alleyways. Don't forget to visit the historic Synagogue of Cordoba and learn about the rich Jewish history of the city.

Dinner (8:00 PM - 10:00 PM):

In the evening, indulge in an authentic Andalusian dinner at a restaurant within the Jewish Quarter. Enjoy local specialties such as "rabos de toro" (oxtail stew) or "salmorejo" and end your day with a taste of Cordoba's cuisine.

Day 2: Royal History and Beautiful Gardens Morning (9:00 AM - 12:00 PM):

Today, explore the Alcázar de los Reyes Cristianos. Stroll through its historic halls, towers, and gardens filled with fountains and sculpted hedges.

Allow yourself time to appreciate the palace's intriguing history.

Lunch (12:30 PM - 2:00 PM):

Head to a local restaurant for a traditional Andalusian lunch, where you can savor dishes like "salmorejo, " "gazpacho, " or "salad with orange and cod. "

Afternoon (2:30 PM - 5:30 PM):

Cross the Roman Bridge (Puente Romano), pausing to take in the panoramic views of the city and the Guadalquivir River. At the far end, you'll find the Calahorra Tower (Torre de la Calahorra), which houses the Museum of Al-Andalus Life. Dive into the fascinating history and culture of Cordoba during Islamic rule.

Dinner (8:00 PM - 10:00 PM):

For dinner, find a charming restaurant along the riverfront, offering a perfect backdrop to enjoy a delightful evening. Savor local delicacies while gazing at the beautifully illuminated landmarks.

Day 3: Courtyards, Palaces, and Botanical Beauty

Morning (9:00 AM - 12:00 PM):

If you're visiting in May during the Patio Festival, start your day by exploring the enchanting Patios of Cordoba (Los Patios de Cordoba). Wander through the beautifully adorned courtyards, each displaying a unique blend of colorful flowers and traditional decorations.

Lunch (12:30 PM - 2:00 PM):

Enjoy a traditional Andalusian lunch at a local restaurant near the courtyards, immersing yourself in the local atmosphere.

Afternoon (2:30 PM - 5:30 PM):

Visit the Palacio de Viana, known as the "Courtyards Palace. " Take your time exploring its 12 charming courtyards, each showcasing distinct architectural features and garden designs.

Dinner (8:00 PM - 10:00 PM):

Choose a cozy restaurant in the heart of Cordoba for a delightful evening meal, where you can indulge in Cordoba's traditional dishes and enjoy the city's evening ambiance.

Day 4: Gardens and Greenery
Morning (9:00 AM - 12:00 PM):

Begin your day with a visit to the Cordoba Botanical Gardens (Jardín Botánico). Meander through the diverse collection of plant species, each representing different climates, and take in the serenity of the gardens.
Lunch (12:30 PM - 2:00 PM):

Enjoy a quick lunch at a local café or restaurant near the gardens, allowing you to continue your exploration.
Afternoon (2:30 PM - 4:30 PM):

Spend your afternoon at leisure. You can choose to shop for souvenirs in the vibrant marketplaces, relax in one of Cordoba's parks, or revisit any of your favorite attractions.

Dinner (8:00 PM - 10:00 PM):

As the sun sets, dine at a charming restaurant serving a mix of local and international cuisine, offering a diverse dining experience..

Day 5: A Plaza and Culinary Delights

Morning (9:00 AM - 12:00 PM):

Start your day at Plaza de la Corredera, a lively square surrounded by colorful buildings. Explore the bustling local market and savor the atmosphere of this historic square.
Lunch (12:30 PM - 2:00 PM):

Enjoy lunch at one of the square's cafes or opt for one of the nearby tapas bars to sample a variety of local dishes.
Afternoon (2:30 PM - 5:30 PM):

Take a leisurely stroll through the city's charming streets, making your way to the Museum of Fine Arts (Museo de Bellas Artes). Explore the museum's impressive collection of Spanish paintings and sculptures, featuring works by renowned artists such as Velázquez and Goya.

Dinner (8:00 PM - 10:00 PM):

Savor a delectable dinner at a local restaurant that specializes in both traditional Andalusian and Spanish cuisine. Enjoy the ambiance of Cordoba's evening as you wrap up the day.

Day 6: Day Trip to Medina Azahara

Morning (9:00 AM - 1:00 PM):

Embark on an exciting day trip to Medina Azahara, a historical archaeological site located just outside Cordoba. Explore the ruins of this medieval palace city, which is a UNESCO World Heritage Site.

Lunch (1:30 PM - 2:30 PM):

Satisfy your hunger with lunch at a nearby restaurant, either within the site or upon your return to Cordoba.

Afternoon (3:00 PM - 6:00 PM):

After returning to Cordoba, visit any attractions you may have missed or revisit your favorites, taking the time to soak in the ambiance of the city.

Dinner (8:00 PM - 10:00 PM):

Conclude your day with a memorable dinner at a local restaurant specializing in traditional Andalusian dishes.

Day 7: Farewell to Cordoba

Morning (9:00 AM - 12:00 PM):

Spend your final morning in Cordoba revisiting any of your favorite sites or exploring new corners of the city. Perhaps take one last stroll through the picturesque courtyards or visit a local market for souvenirs.

Lunch (12:30 PM - 2:00 PM):

Savor your last Spanish meal at a local restaurant, making sure to enjoy some of the local delicacies one last time.

Afternoon (2:30 PM - 4:30 PM):

Reflect on your Cordoba journey with a visit to a local café for a cup of Spanish coffee or dessert, while you recall the highlights of your trip.

As your 7-day adventure in Cordoba comes to a close, you'll leave with cherished memories of this enchanting city, where history, culture, and beauty converge to create an unforgettable travel experience. Cordoba is a place where the past and present harmoniously blend, making it a perfect destination for those seeking a rich and diverse cultural experience.

TOP BEACHES CORDOBA.

Here are some of the top beaches in Cordoba:

Playa de la Almadraba:

Located just 15 kilometers (9 miles) from the city center, Playa de la Almadraba offers a peaceful escape from the hustle and bustle of Cordoba. This riverside beach along the Guadalquivir River is known for its clear waters, ideal for swimming and kayaking. The backdrop of olive groves and rolling hills adds to the tranquility.

Playa de Posadas:

A short drive west from Cordoba takes you to Playa de Posadas, a popular spot for locals and visitors alike. This man-made beach is nestled alongside the Posadas reservoir, creating a serene environment for sunbathing and picnicking. The surrounding pine trees provide shade, making it a perfect destination for a leisurely day out.

Playa de la Colada:

Situated on the banks of the Guadalquivir River, Playa de la Colada is a beautiful, sandy escape that offers relaxation and natural beauty. It's perfect for those who wish to enjoy a day at the "beach" while staying close to Cordoba. The clear river waters are inviting for a refreshing swim.

Embalse de Zufre Beach:

A bit farther afield, approximately a 2-hour drive from Cordoba, lies the Embalse de Zufre. This artificial reservoir surrounded by hills offers a refreshing respite. The beach here is excellent for swimming, and the lush landscape is ideal for a picnic.

Playa del Parador de Mazagón:

If you're willing to take a scenic drive towards the coast, about a 3-hour drive from Cordoba, you'll find Playa del Parador de Mazagón. This vast sandy beach along the Atlantic Ocean is perfect for those seeking the classic beach experience. Sunbathe, swim, and enjoy the sea breeze. Mazagón is also known for its fresh seafood restaurants.

Playa de Punta Umbría:

Just a bit further southwest, a 3. 5-hour drive from Cordoba, is Playa de Punta Umbría, a popular beach town known for its extensive sandy shores and vibrant atmosphere. The beach is flanked by restaurants, bars, and shops, making it a great destination for a day of sun and sea

OUTDOOR ACTIVITIES IN CORDOBA.

Cordoba is a city that effortlessly balances its rich historical heritage with a vibrant, modern lifestyle. While the city's historical and architectural wonders are undoubtedly captivating, Cordoba also offers a plethora of outdoor activities for those who seek to embrace the natural beauty and adventure that surrounds this historic gem. In this chapter, we'll delve into the diverse and exciting outdoor experiences that Cordoba has to offer, from leisurely strolls along the Guadalquivir River to adrenaline-pumping adventures in the nearby Sierra Morena mountains.

1. Exploring the Riverside Promenade:

Begin your outdoor escapades in Cordoba with a leisurely walk or bike ride along the picturesque riverside promenade. The Guadalquivir River, with its gently flowing waters, provides a serene backdrop for your exploration. You can rent bikes or simply take a relaxing stroll while admiring the views. This area also features parks, gardens, and exercise spots for those who want to stay active.

2. Sierra Morena Hiking and Nature Trails:

For nature enthusiasts and hikers, the Sierra Morena mountain range beckons just north of Cordoba. These rugged and forested hills are a haven for outdoor adventurers. A variety of well-marked trails cater to different levels of expertise, whether you're a seasoned hiker or just looking for a casual nature walk. The Sierra Morena offers not only stunning natural landscapes but also the opportunity to spot local wildlife and enjoy the fresh mountain air.

3. Birdwatching in the Wetlands:

The natural wetlands and marshes surrounding Cordoba provide a haven for birdwatching enthusiasts. Species like flamingos, herons, and egrets can be spotted in the region. The Laguna de Zóñar and the Laguna del Rincón are two notable birdwatching spots, where you can observe these magnificent creatures in their natural habitat. Consider bringing binoculars and a field guide to make the most of this experience.

4. Horseback Riding in the Countryside:

Experience the charm of Cordoba's countryside with a horseback ride through olive groves and rolling hills. Various local operators offer guided tours that can cater to all levels of riders. It's a unique way to soak in the Andalusian landscape while bonding with these majestic animals.

5. Adventure Sports in the Sierra Morena:

For adrenaline junkies, the Sierra Morena presents opportunities for rock climbing, mountain biking, and even zip-lining. There are adventure tour companies in Cordoba that can arrange guided outings, ensuring both safety and excitement. Whether you're a novice or an experienced adventurer, the Sierra Morena has something for everyone.

6. Kayaking on the Guadalquivir:

Paddle your way through Cordoba's waterways with a kayaking adventure on the Guadalquivir River. Rentals and guided tours are available, offering a unique perspective of the city and its surroundings. This activity is both refreshing and provides excellent photo opportunities.

7. Picnicking and Botanical Gardens:

For a more relaxed outdoor experience, consider a picnic in Cordoba's lovely parks, such as the Gardens of the Alcázar. Alternatively, explore the city's botanical gardens and soak in the beauty of exotic and native plants.

8. Hot Air Balloon Ride:

See Cordoba from a completely different angle by taking a hot air balloon ride over the city and its surroundings. This unforgettable experience offers panoramic views, particularly during sunrise or sunset, when the city is bathed in golden hues.

9. Cycling the Greenway of the Campiña:

Explore the scenic countryside around Cordoba by cycling along the Greenway of the Campiña, a converted railway line. This flat and well-maintained route takes you through picturesque rural landscapes, allowing you to appreciate the region's agricultural heritage.

10. Stargazing in Sierra Morena:

The Sierra Morena's clear skies make it an ideal location for stargazing. Consider joining an astronomy tour to observe the constellations and celestial wonders that light up the night.

As you explore these outdoor activities in and around Cordoba, you'll discover a city that offers not only historical riches but also the beauty of its natural surroundings. Cordoba is a destination where adventure and tranquility coexist harmoniously, providing a well-rounded travel experience for all. Whether you're an avid adventurer, a nature lover, or simply seeking a breath of fresh air, Cordoba's outdoor offerings are sure to leave a lasting impression on your journey through this enchanting Spanish city.

10 DELICIOUS DISHES YOU SHOULD TRY WHEN YOU VISIT CORDOBA

Cordoba is not only a city steeped in history and architectural wonders but also a place where your taste buds can embark on a delectable journey through its rich culinary heritage. One of the most intriguing and delicious aspects of Cordoba is its traditional cuisine, which combines flavors from Andalusia and the Mediterranean. Here are ten mouthwatering dishes that you must savor when you visit this enchanting city:

Salmorejo:

A close cousin to gazpacho, this cold, velvety soup is a local favorite. What makes it intriguing is the texture - it's creamier and thicker than gazpacho, owing to the use of bread and ripe tomatoes. It's often garnished with diced hard-boiled eggs and jamón serrano (Spanish cured ham).

Flamenquín:

Cordoba's version of the chicken or ham schnitzel, the flamenquín is a tasty treat wrapped in ham and cheese, breaded and deep-fried to crispy perfection. It's a delight for both young and old.

Rabo de Toro:

If you're feeling adventurous, try this Andalusian delicacy. Cordoba's rabo de toro is a stew made from bull's tail, slow-cooked until it's tender and flavorful, often served with a rich wine sauce.

Berza Cordobesa:

This hearty stew combines chickpeas, chorizo, morcilla (blood sausage), and vegetables. It's an intriguing and satisfying dish, perfect for filling up after a day of exploration.

Salmorejo Cordobés:

You might think you know salmorejo, but Cordoba's version is extra special. What sets it apart is the use of locally grown tomatoes and a generous drizzle of top-quality olive oil, creating a true Andalusian delight.

Espinacas con Garbanzos:

A simple yet delicious dish, this combines spinach, chickpeas, and a blend of spices. It's both nutritious and delightful, with a flavor that has been perfected over centuries.

Mazamorra:

An intriguing dessert, mazamorra is a sweet porridge made from ground almonds, milk, sugar, and cinnamon. It's often served with a drizzle of honey and is the perfect ending to a Cordoban meal.

Salchichón de Pozo Blanco:

Cordoba is renowned for its sausages, and the salchichón de Pozo Blanco is a particular local favorite. It's a flavorful, cured sausage, perfect for snacking or enjoying with cheese and wine.

Pastel Cordobés:

An intriguing pastry that's both sweet and savory. This pie is filled with a mixture of sugar, almonds, squash, and anise, and is a traditional dessert during Cordoba's annual Fair.

Ajoblanco:

A refreshing, chilled soup made from ground almonds, garlic, and olive oil, ajoblanco is perfect for cooling down on a hot Cordoban day. It's traditionally garnished with grapes or melon.

Cordoba's culinary scene is a delightful blend of tradition and innovation, and trying these dishes will provide you with a deep appreciation for the city's unique gastronomy. Whether you're a food lover or a curious traveler, exploring Cordoba's intriguing and delicious dishes is an essential part of your journey through this enchanting city.

TOP 10 HOTELS IN CORDOBA

Hospes Palacio del Bailío:

Located in a beautifully restored 16th-century palace, Hospes Palacio del Bailío offers a luxurious experience in the heart of Cordoba. The hotel boasts stunning courtyards, a spa, and a gourmet restaurant. Each room is elegantly decorated, combining historic charm with modern comfort.

Eurostars Palace:

Eurostars Palace is a contemporary 5-star hotel with an excellent location near the Mezquita. The sleek design, rooftop pool, and panoramic views of the city make it a popular choice for travelers seeking both comfort and convenience.

NH Collection Amistad Cordoba:

This historic hotel is set within two 18th-century mansions and is just a stone's throw from the Mezquita. It offers a harmonious blend of traditional Andalusian architecture and modern amenities, making it a favorite for those looking to explore Cordoba on foot.

Las Casas de la Judería:

Nestled in the heart of the Jewish Quarter, Las Casas de la Judería is a unique collection of interconnected townhouses, creating a labyrinth of courtyards, patios, and gardens. It's like stepping into a medieval Spanish village.

Balcón de Córdoba:

Overlooking the Mezquita, Balcón de Córdoba offers a delightful and romantic ambiance. This boutique hotel is known for its intimate courtyard, elegant rooms, and a rooftop terrace that provides breathtaking views of the city's iconic landmarks.

Casa de los Azulejos:

Housed in a beautifully restored 18th-century mansion, Casa de los Azulejos is known for its stunning blue-and-white tilework. The hotel exudes historical charm, with cozy rooms and a serene courtyard, making it an oasis of tranquility in the city.

Hotel Madinat:

This boutique hotel offers an Arabian Nights ambiance with a modern touch. It's located within walking distance of the Mezquita and features stylish rooms, a lovely garden, and a welcoming staff that goes above and beyond to make your stay memorable.

Hotel Viento10:

A contemporary hotel situated in the heart of Cordoba, Hotel Viento10 stands out for its sleek design, rooftop terrace, and splendid views of the Mezquita. It's a perfect choice for travelers who appreciate modern comfort.

Casa Maika:

This charming, family-run guesthouse is located in the Jewish Quarter and offers a cozy and personalized experience. The warm hospitality, delightful rooms, and a lovely patio make it a home away from home for many guests.

Hotel San Miguel:

Hotel San Miguel is a budget-friendly option offering comfortable and clean rooms. Its central location allows guests to explore Cordoba's major attractions on foot. The hotel provides excellent value for money without sacrificing quality.

These top 10 hotels in Cordoba cater to a wide range of tastes and budgets. Whether you seek historical charm, modern luxury, or a cozy boutique experience, there's an ideal choice for every traveler. Including these hotels in your Cordoba travel guide will help visitors make informed decisions when selecting their accommodations in this captivating city

TOP TRAVEL RESOURCES FOR MAKING RESERVATIONS

In the digital age, planning a trip to Cordoba, Spain, has never been easier thanks to the plethora of travel resources available to modern travelers. Whether you're seeking accommodations, flights, or activities, the year 2024 is a prime time to harness the power of technology to make your Cordoba travel reservations. In this chapter, we'll delve into the top travel resources for securing the best reservations and experiences in Cordoba, offering a mix of online platforms, mobile apps, and local recommendations to ensure your trip is seamless and unforgettable.

1. Booking. com: As one of the world's leading online accommodation platforms, Booking. com offers an extensive range of hotels, hostels, and apartments in Cordoba. The platform allows you to filter your search based on price, location, and user reviews, providing a vast array of options to suit any budget and travel style.

2. Airbnb: For those seeking a more authentic experience, Airbnb is an ideal resource for finding unique accommodations in Cordoba, including apartments and homes that immerse you in the local culture. This platform often offers a chance to stay in historic buildings with Cordoba's unmistakable Andalusian charm.

3. Expedia: Expedia is a comprehensive platform for booking flights, hotels, and rental cars. It's an excellent choice for travelers who prefer bundling their reservations to save money.

4. Hostelworld: If you're a budget traveler or prefer a social atmosphere, Hostelworld is your go-to resource for finding and reserving hostels in Cordoba. This platform provides detailed descriptions, photos, and traveler reviews to help you make an informed decision.

5. Cordoba Tourism Office: While online resources are essential, don't underestimate the value of local information. The Cordoba Tourism Office, situated in the heart of the city, can provide

recommendations for accommodations and help you secure reservations.

6. Skyscanner: When it comes to finding flights, Skyscanner is an invaluable resource. It allows you to compare flight options from different airlines, find the best deals, and conveniently book your tickets.

7. Rome2rio: Rome2rio is a fantastic tool for planning your travel within Cordoba and to and from the city. This resource provides information on various transportation options, including buses, trains, and flights.

8. Viator: For organizing tours and activities in Cordoba, Viator is a trusted platform. It offers a wide range of experiences, from guided tours of Cordoba's historic landmarks to immersive cultural activities.

9. TripAdvisor: TripAdvisor is an excellent resource for reading reviews and gaining insights from fellow travelers. It can help you choose the

best restaurants, attractions, and accommodations in Cordoba.

10. Google Maps: Don't forget the power of Google Maps for navigating Cordoba. This app provides real-time directions, public transportation information, and reviews for local businesses, making it an indispensable tool for travelers.

These top travel resources for making reservations in Cordoba in 2024 cover all aspects of trip planning, from accommodations and flights to activities and transportation. By utilizing these resources, you can ensure a smooth and enjoyable visit to this captivating Andalusian city. Whether you're a solo traveler, a couple, or a family, Cordoba awaits with open arms, and these tools will help you make the most of your journey.

CONCLUSION

As your journey through this Cordoba Travel Guide culminates, you've traversed an expedition across time, culture, and history that will linger in your memory for years to come. Cordoba, the gem of Andalusia, offers an experience that is nothing short of enchanting. The captivating mysteries of this city, revealed through its geographical marvels, rich historical tapestry, and vibrant contemporary culture, have transformed your visit into an indelible odyssey.

You've stood in awe within the sacred confines of the Great Mosque of Cordoba, where Islamic artistry and Catholic devotion coalesce in an architectural symphony. The Alcázar de los Reyes Cristianos has murmured tales of monarchs and heroes through its centuries-old walls, while the labyrinthine streets of the Jewish Quarter have invited you to become immersed in their romantic ambience.

As you crossed the ancient Roman Bridge and gazed at the reflection of Cordoba in the tranquil waters of the Guadalquivir, you felt the pulse of this city, resonating with the echoes of past civilizations. The Calahorra Tower stood sentinel-like, unveiling the resilience of Cordoba's people and their enduring cultural legacy.

The Palacio de Viana's courtyards transported you to a bygone era of opulence and beauty, each one a living work of art. The Cordoba Botanical Gardens provided a serene retreat amidst the city's hustle and bustle, a place for rejuvenation and reflection.

At Plaza de la Corredera, you immersed yourself in the spirited atmosphere of Cordoba, engaging with locals and fellow travelers alike. The Cordoba's Patios festival in May introduced you to the warmth and hospitality of Cordobans, as their homes bloomed with vibrant flora and welcoming smiles.

Within the hallowed halls of the Museum of Fine Arts, you marveled at Spain's artistic heritage, encapsulated in timeless masterpieces that spoke of the nation's essence.

Cordoba's allure is not merely superficial; it resides in the rhythms of flamenco that saturate the air, the tapas that tantalize your palate, and the spirit of the May Crosses Festival that saturates the city with joy. Cordoba is a city that venerates its past while embracing its future.

As you take your final promenade through the historic streets of Cordoba, you carry with you not just a travel guide but a treasury of memories, a sense of wonder, and the reverberations of history that eternally bind this city to your heart. Cordoba is more than a mere location; it's an experience that transcends time and place, leaving an indelible imprint on your soul.

So, as you bid adieu to Cordoba, remember that this bewitching city will forever remain a part of you. May the pages of this guide serve as an enduring portal, allowing you to revisit the wonders of Cordoba whenever you desire. With the anticipation that your adventures will persist and you'll explore novel horizons, we bid you adieu, traveler. Until we cross paths again, in Cordoba or in spirit, safe travels, and may the world continue to astonish and inspire you.

Printed in Great Britain
by Amazon